MW01289024

The
Sobriety Journal

To Feel Better Every Day

CREATED BY:

Joanne Edmund

Disclaimer

This book is not intended to act as a substitute for medical advice or treatment. Any person with a condition requiring medical attention should consult a qualified medical practitioner or suitable therapist. The information provided in this book is stated to be truthful and consistent, in that any liability, in terms of inattention or otherwise, by any usage or abuse of any policies, processes, or directions contained within is the solitary and utter responsibility of the recipient reader. Under no circumstances will any legal responsibility or blame be held against the publisher for any reparation, damages, or monetary loss due to the information herein, either directly or indirectly.

**If you don't want to sink,
you better figure out how to swim.**

Jeannette Walls, *The Glass Castle*

INTRODUCTION

Thousands and thousands of words full of tears. It was in those darkest moments, when the thunder of my drinking problem set me on fire, that I somehow found a way to write. To push out all my anger, lost dreams and fear into the tiny pages of my notebook. When, many drinks later, I started to find sobriety it was to those blank pages I returned. My pen functioning as the bridge between my thoughts and the white lined paper. While writing, for the first time in a long, dark period, I found a sense of control. I found my sword against the drunken demons.

When I finished **Quit Drinking**, *And Inspiring Alcohol Recovery Workbook* last year, it stumbled upon me that I had made an enormous step towards lasting sobriety. I had found a use for my addictive years. Sharing the lessons of both my pain and hopes. I did not know what to expect, but so far I feel enormous joy when I realised how many people have already bought my book. Sometimes I pray at night that for those out there, seeking a solution, my recovery book can serve as a little candle of hope and inspiration.

Then, one morning while reading my journals of the past year, I realised how ordering my thoughts and reminding myself of being grateful was such an important part of my recovery. I knew that my next book shouldn't be another classic self-help book, or a drinking memoir; no it had to be something practical and encouraging. Thus, I created together with the True Potential Project team, *The Sobriety Journal.* Of course, it is important to seek wisdom outside yourself. Learn from others through meetings, counselling, YouTube videos and self-help books. But what about the wisdom that is inside you? What about the lessons you learnt during your life? A practical way to find your wisdom, learn from it and make silent progression in the meantime is through journaling.

The Sobriety Journal gives you a chance to fit journaling into your daily routine. With five daily questions, three for the morning and two for at night, you will go on an inward journey of wisdom, gratitude, learning and happiness. May journaling make as big a difference in your life as it did in mine!

On the next page I will explain how you can use this journal.

How To Use This Journal

This Journal consists of five question. Three for the morning and two for your evening routine.
These are the questions:

MORNING
If I did this, today would be great.

How could I help myself today?

My affirmation for today.

EVENING
What did I learn today?

What made me grateful today?

Every page consists of these five questions. With so much as five minutes per morning and five minutes per evening you can make this journal an easy to follow daily habit that will enrich your life. Start journaling when it feels most convenient to you. For example, just after breakfast and right before you go to work. Most importantly, do it at a consistent time.

Then, the questions. How could you answer them? Of course this is up to you, but I will give an example for all of these questions.

If I did this, today would be great.

Instead of making a big, intimidating to-do-list, write down one or two major goals that would make your day perfect. Make a commitment that you know you can keep. Get into the habit of knowing that you can count on yourself. An example:

Writing 500 words for my new novel.

How could I help myself today?

Instead of criticizing yourself and being negative, what is it that you could do to help yourself today? How could you help yourself through the day, enjoying the day and doing the necessary tasks? An example:

Every time I start to criticize myself, I will ask the question: how can I encourage myself more positively?

My affirmation for today.

A statement that you will live your day by. Possibly this affirmation is going to be the same some of the days. That is okay, repetition is power. An example:

I am a unique human being and do not compare myself to others.

EVENING

What did I learn today?

Everyday life grants us with life lessons which are way more precious than what we could ever learn in school Try to recognize these lessons. Pay attention and make progress. An example:

Setting intimidating goals gives me stress and doesn't produce the desired results.

What made me grateful today?

There is so much to be grateful for each day, but sometime it is hard to see. The beauty of life is often caught through clouds of worries and circumstances. But when you try to remember, the good things will come up easily. An example:

The smile on the face of my good friend, when meeting her.

Every 7 days there is a short text that you can use for inspiration at the start of a new week. Over time your journal will be a short autobiography that you can reflect on for years to come. Because a life worth living is a life worth recording.

On the next page, you can set your daily journaling time.

Your Journaling Habit

Now, pick a time you will generally do your journaling. Also pick a desired place where you could do the journaling. When you pick a time and place for your habit, it will be more likely that you will follow through with it. Of course, there are times when you can't follow it exactly. But when you have consciously picked and created your habit, it will be easier to get back on track soon.

Every morning I will journal:

_____

_____

_____

_____

Example: Right after breakfast at the dinner table.

Every evening I will journal:

_____

_____

_____

_____

Example: Just before I go to bed, at the desk in my bedroom.

The
Sobriety Journal

Fear and pain should be treated as signals not to close our eyes
but to open them wider.

Nathaniel Branden

> **We cannot change anything**
> **if we cannot change our thinking.**
>
> Santosh Kalwar

DATE: _____-_____-_____

If I did this, today would be great.

_____
_____

How could I help myself today?

_____
_____
_____

My affirmation for today.

_____
_____

EVENING

What did I learn today?

_____
_____
_____
_____

What made me grateful today?

_____
_____
_____

It does not do to dwell on dreams
and forget to live.

J.K. Rowling

DATE: _____-_____-_____

If I did this, today would be great.

_____

_____

How could I help myself today?

_____

_____

_____

My affirmation for today.

_____

_____

EVENING

What did I learn today?

_____

_____

_____

_____

What made me grateful today?

_____

_____

_____

Tell me, what is it you plan to do with your one wild and precious life?

Mary Oliver

DATE: _____-_____-_____

If I did this, today would be great.

How could I help myself today?

My affirmation for today.

EVENING

What did I learn today?

What made me grateful today?

I have loved the stars too fondly
to be fearful of the night.

Sarah Williams

DATE: ____-____-_____

If I did this, today would be great.

_____

_____

How could I help myself today?

_____

_____

_____

My affirmation for today.

_____

_____

EVENING

What did I learn today?

_____

_____

_____

_____

What made me grateful today?

_____

_____

_____

> What is that you express in your eyes? It seems to me more than all the print I have read in my life.

Walt Whitman

DATE: ____-____-_____

If I did this, today would be great.

_____

How could I help myself today?

_____

My affirmation for today.

_____

EVENING

What did I learn today?

_____

What made me grateful today?

_____

> I shut my eyes and all the world drops dead;
> I lift my eyes and all is born again.

Sylvia Plath

DATE: _____-_____-_____

If I did this, today would be great.

_____

_____

How could I help myself today?

_____

_____

_____

My affirmation for today.

_____

EVENING

What did I learn today?

_____

_____

_____

_____

What made me grateful today?

_____

_____

_____

> The possession of knowledge does not kill the sense of
> wonder and mystery. There is always more mystery.

Anais Nin

DATE: _____-_____-_____

If I did this, today would be great.

How could I help myself today?

My affirmation for today.

EVENING

What did I learn today?

What made me grateful today?

Love

What has made it all worth it? I asked myself this question once, when I felt down and out. Beaten down by days of drinking, I was leading myself into a dark and stinking pit of destruction.

Then, one night, only partly conscious, I lay down on the smelly sheets of my bed. I was alone. My curtains were closed and only vaguely I heard the noise of cars passing by. A question found its way through my spinning head;

'What has made it all worth it?'

And while lying in bed, seeing no future, about to give up, that question kept spinning. A leaf on a stormy autumn day. Memories came, pain, grief, but soon they were gone and changed by the better moments. I saw the people I cared for, the smiles, the hugs, the connection. I recalled conversations and moments of joy. Tears came, because I understood that the past wasn't just the past. That those moments weren't just a memory. They were a promise that life was worthwhile.

I had a dream that night about clear water, flowers and dolphins. The following morning I realized that something had changed. A seed of hope was planted.

> Those who are willing to be vulnerable
> move among mysteries.
>
> Theodore Roethke

DATE: ____-____-_____

If I did this, today would be great.

_____

_____

How could I help myself today?

_____

_____

_____

_____

My affirmation for today.

_____

_____

EVENING

What did I learn today?

_____

_____

_____

_____

What made me grateful today?

_____

_____

_____

Without deviation from the norm, progress is not possible.

Frank Zappa

DATE: _____-_____-_____

If I did this, today would be great.

_____

_____

How could I help myself today?

_____

_____

_____

_____

My affirmation for today.

_____

_____

EVENING

What did I learn today?

_____

_____

_____

_____

What made me grateful today?

_____

_____

_____

If you ever find yourself in the wrong story, leave.

Mo Willems

DATE: _____-_____-_____

If I did this, today would be great.

_____

_____

How could I help myself today?

_____

_____

_____

_____

My affirmation for today.

_____

_____

EVENING

What did I learn today?

_____

_____

_____

_____

_____

What made me grateful today?

_____

_____

_____

The past has no power
over the present moment.

Eckhart Tolle

DATE: _____-_____-_____

If I did this, today would be great.

How could I help myself today?

My affirmation for today.

EVENING

What did I learn today?

What made me grateful today?

When we are tired,
we are attacked by ideas we conquered long ago.

Friedrich Nietzsche

DATE: _____-_____-_____

If I did this, today would be great.

_____
_____

How could I help myself today?

_____
_____
_____
_____

My affirmation for today.

_____
_____

EVENING

What did I learn today?

_____
_____
_____
_____

What made me grateful today?

_____
_____
_____

Like all magnificent things,
it's very simple.

Natalie Babbitt

DATE: ____-____-_____

If I did this, today would be great.

_____

_____

How could I help myself today?

_____

_____

_____

My affirmation for today.

_____

_____

EVENING

What did I learn today?

_____

_____

_____

_____

What made me grateful today?

_____

_____

_____

It is not true that people stop pursuing dreams because they grow old, they grow old because they stop pursuing dreams.

Gabriel García Márquez

DATE: _____-_____-_____

If I did this, today would be great.

_____
_____

How could I help myself today?

_____
_____
_____
_____

My affirmation for today.

_____
_____

EVENING

What did I learn today?

_____
_____
_____
_____

What made me grateful today?

_____
_____
_____

Addiction & Learning

If everything in life has a purpose, what was the purpose of your drinking problem? Was the drinking really the problem, or was it the pain you needed to numb? It has taken me a long time, but now I am no longer reflecting on my addiction with rage. Of course I still have many regrets, but more and more I begin to realize that my alcoholism served its purpose.It helped me to run away from the deep traumatic pain that was too hard for me to bear. No, it absolutely wasn't the best way to cope with it, but it was the only remedy I knew.

Now, with the distance that time always grants us, I watch my drinking years with more compassion. If I could turn back the hands of time, yes, I guess I would. I not only hurt myself, I hurt the one I love the most.

And I guess that always happens with destruction...

But to be angry at myself or at my addiction isn't the right way. Understanding my addictive behavior has given me peace. It wasn't the drinking that was the core problem, it was the pain that I needed to numb.

I sincerely hope that during your recovery you will find the source of your alcoholism and heal the pain. Simply quitting your addiction isn't enough. It is a coping mechanism for dealing with (deep) pain.

So eventually, that is what needs to be addressed: the source, the pain.

> There are moments when we resort to senseless formulations
> and advance absurd claims to hide straightforward feelings.

Elena Ferrante

DATE: _____-_____-_____

If I did this, today would be great.

_____

_____

How could I help myself today?

_____

_____

_____

My affirmation for today.

_____

_____

EVENING

What did I learn today?

_____

_____

_____

_____

What made me grateful today?

_____

_____

_____

> One does not become enlightened by imagining figures of light, but by making the darkness conscious.

Carl Gustav Jung

DATE: ____-____-_____

If I did this, today would be great.

_____

_____

How could I help myself today?

_____

_____

_____

_____

My affirmation for today.

_____

_____

EVENING

What did I learn today?

_____

_____

_____

_____

What made me grateful today?

_____

_____

_____

Never be afraid to trust an unknown future to a known God.

Corrie ten Boom

DATE: _____-_____-_____

If I did this, today would be great.

_____

_____

How could I help myself today?

_____

_____

_____

_____

My affirmation for today.

_____

_____

EVENING

What did I learn today?

_____

_____

_____

_____

What made me grateful today?

_____

_____

_____

> I know you want to question everything,
> but sometimes it pays to just have a little faith.

Lauren Kate

DATE: _____-_____-_____

If I did this, today would be great.

_____

_____

How could I help myself today?

_____

_____

_____

_____

My affirmation for today.

_____

_____

EVENING

What did I learn today?

_____

_____

_____

_____

What made me grateful today?

_____

_____

_____

Be kind,
for everyone you meet is fighting a hard battle.

Socrates

DATE: _____-_____-_____

If I did this, today would be great.

_____

_____

How could I help myself today?

_____

_____

_____

My affirmation for today.

_____

EVENING

What did I learn today?

_____

_____

_____

What made me grateful today?

_____

_____

The poetry of the earth
is never dead.

John Keats

DATE: _____-_____-_____

If I did this, today would be great.

_____

_____

How could I help myself today?

_____

_____

_____

My affirmation for today.

_____

_____

EVENING

What did I learn today?

_____

_____

_____

_____

What made me grateful today?

_____

_____

_____

**Do not be afraid; our fate Cannot be taken from us;
it is a gift.**

Dante Alighieri

DATE: ____-____-_____

If I did this, today would be great.

_____
_____

How could I help myself today?

_____
_____
_____
_____

My affirmation for today.

_____
_____

EVENING

What did I learn today?

_____
_____
_____
_____
_____

What made me grateful today?

_____
_____
_____

Courage

One meaning of the word 'courage' is ' strength in the face of pain or grief'. Trying to quit something that has been a habit for many years is an act of courage. Bravery. Know the strength inside yourself. The power that has guided you to make the tough decision to break the destructive spell. It is what characterizes you; strength in the face of pain or grief.

> What drains your spirit drains your body.
> What fuels your spirit fuels your body.
>
> Carolyn Myss

DATE: _____-_____-_____

If I did this, today would be great.

_____

_____

How could I help myself today?

_____

_____

_____

_____

My affirmation for today.

_____

_____

EVENING

What did I learn today?

_____

_____

_____

_____

What made me grateful today?

_____

_____

_____

Change the way you look at things
and the things you look at change.

Wayne W. Dyer

DATE: _____-_____-_____

If I did this, today would be great.

_____

_____

How could I help myself today?

_____

_____

_____

_____

My affirmation for today.

_____

EVENING

What did I learn today?

_____

_____

_____

_____

_____

What made me grateful today?

_____

_____

_____

It is bizarre to treat all differences
as oppositions

Kate Chopin

DATE: _____-_____-_____

If I did this, today would be great.

_____

_____

How could I help myself today?

_____

_____

_____

My affirmation for today.

_____

_____

EVENING

What did I learn today?

_____

_____

_____

_____

What made me grateful today?

_____

_____

_____

There is peace
even in the storm.

Vincent van Gogh

DATE: ____-____-_____

If I did this, today would be great.

_____

_____

How could I help myself today?

_____

_____

_____

_____

My affirmation for today.

_____

_____

EVENING

What did I learn today?

_____

_____

_____

_____

What made me grateful today?

_____

_____

_____

> You wanna fly,
> you got to give up the shit that weighs you down.

Toni Morrison

DATE: ____-____-_____

If I did this, today would be great.

_____

_____

How could I help myself today?

_____

_____

_____

My affirmation for today.

_____

_____

EVENING

What did I learn today?

_____

_____

_____

_____

What made me grateful today?

_____

_____

_____

Nothing contributes so much to tranquilize the mind as a steady purpose.

Mary Shelley

DATE: ____-____-_____

If I did this, today would be great.

_____

_____

How could I help myself today?

_____

_____

_____

_____

My affirmation for today.

_____

_____

EVENING

What did I learn today?

_____

_____

_____

_____

What made me grateful today?

_____

_____

_____

It is never too late
to be what you might have been.

George Eliot

DATE: ____-____-_____

If I did this, today would be great.

How could I help myself today?

My affirmation for today.

EVENING

What did I learn today?

What made me grateful today?

Inspiration

A big part of my life, ever since I've been in recovery, is seeking the right inspiration. I try to surround myself with information and people that bring out the best in me. Books, YouTube videos, recovery support groups, coaching, and it goes on. Just like eating, your mental diet is important for your psychological health.

> Life appears to me too short
> to be spent in nursing animosity or registering wrongs.

Charlotte Bronte

DATE: ____-____-_____

If I did this, today would be great.

How could I help myself today?

My affirmation for today.

EVENING

What did I learn today?

What made me grateful today?

> Doing less is not being lazy. Don't give in to a culture
> that values personal sacrifice over personal productivity.

Tim Ferriss

DATE: _____-_____-_____

If I did this, today would be great.

_____

_____

How could I help myself today?

_____

_____

_____

_____

My affirmation for today.

_____

_____

EVENING

What did I learn today?

_____

_____

_____

_____

What made me grateful today?

_____

_____

_____

> **When I let go of what I am,**
> **I become what I might be.**
>
> Lao Tzu

DATE: ____-____-_____

If I did this, today would be great.

How could I help myself today?

My affirmation for today.

EVENING

What did I learn today?

What made me grateful today?

> It's not a question of learning much. On the contrary.
> It's a question of UNLEARNING much.

Osho

DATE: ____-____-_____

If I did this, today would be great.

_____

_____

How could I help myself today?

_____

_____

_____

_____

My affirmation for today.

_____

_____

EVENING

What did I learn today?

_____

_____

_____

_____

What made me grateful today?

_____

_____

_____

Don't let the bastards
grind you down.

Margaret Atwood

DATE: _____-_____-_____

If I did this, today would be great.

_____
_____

How could I help myself today?

_____
_____
_____
_____

My affirmation for today.

_____
_____

EVENING

What did I learn today?

_____
_____
_____
_____

What made me grateful today?

_____
_____
_____

> Happiness was like a green vine spreading through her,
> stretching fine tendrils, bearing flowers through her flesh.

Patricia Highsmith

DATE: _____-_____-_____

If I did this, today would be great.

_____

_____

How could I help myself today?

_____

_____

_____

_____

My affirmation for today.

_____

_____

EVENING

What did I learn today?

_____

_____

_____

_____

What made me grateful today?

_____

_____

_____

> And from the midst of cheerless gloom
> I passed to bright unclouded day.

Emily Bronte

DATE: _____-_____-_____

If I did this, today would be great.

_____

_____

How could I help myself today?

_____

_____

_____

My affirmation for today.

_____

_____

EVENING

What did I learn today?

_____

_____

_____

_____

What made me grateful today?

_____

_____

_____

Passion

As a young girl, I wanted to be a writer. Creating far away worlds. And I wrote, I wrote a lot. Then came the alcohol. Then the addiction. But the dream, it stayed. It was safely hidden from the claws of my drunkness.

However for years I never wrote constantly, like I did in my youth. My energy and self confidence were derailed. Over the last three years I have picked up my writing again. I realized during my recovery that as a human being you are meant to develop your God given talents, even if they seem insignificant or small. It helps when you work on something you just enjoy. I started small, sometimes no more than 100 words a day. But I followed through, and writing brought light to my darker days.

Now it has a developed into a precious daily habit, one that I look forward to and take care of.

I did then what I knew how to do.
Now that I know better, I do better.

Maya Angelou

DATE: _____-_____-_____

If I did this, today would be great.

How could I help myself today?

My affirmation for today.

EVENING

What did I learn today?

What made me grateful today?

Until we can receive with an open heart,
we are never really giving with an open heart.

Brene Brown

DATE: _____-_____-_____

If I did this, today would be great.

_____

_____

How could I help myself today?

_____

_____

_____

_____

My affirmation for today.

_____

_____

EVENING

What did I learn today?

_____

_____

_____

_____

What made me grateful today?

_____

_____

_____

> Love makes your soul crawl out
> from its hiding place.

Zora Neale Hurston

DATE: _____-_____-_____

If I did this, today would be great.

_____

_____

How could I help myself today?

_____

_____

_____

_____

My affirmation for today.

_____

_____

EVENING

What did I learn today?

_____

_____

_____

_____

What made me grateful today?

_____

_____

_____

> It is in your moments of decision
> that your destiny is shaped.

Anthony Robbins

If I did this, today would be great.

_____

_____

How could I help myself today?

_____

_____

_____

_____

My affirmation for today.

_____

_____

EVENING

What did I learn today?

_____

_____

_____

_____

What made me grateful today?

_____

_____

_____

I am not afraid of storms,
for I am learning how to sail my ship.

Louisa May Alcott

DATE: _____-_____-_____

If I did this, today would be great.

_____

_____

How could I help myself today?

_____

_____

_____

My affirmation for today.

_____

_____

EVENING

What did I learn today?

_____

_____

_____

_____

What made me grateful today?

_____

_____

_____

The soul becomes dyed
with the colour of its thoughts.

Marcus Aurelius

DATE: _____-_____-_____

If I did this, today would be great.

_____

_____

How could I help myself today?

_____

_____

_____

_____

My affirmation for today.

_____

_____

EVENING

What did I learn today?

_____

_____

_____

_____

What made me grateful today?

_____

_____

_____

I think you travel to search
and you come back home to find yourself there.

Chimamanda Ngozi Adichie

DATE: ____-____-_____

If I did this, today would be great.

_____

_____

How could I help myself today?

_____

_____

_____

_____

My affirmation for today.

_____

_____

EVENING

What did I learn today?

_____

_____

_____

_____

What made me grateful today?

_____

_____

_____

Secrets

During our addiction, we tend to keep our bad habits as good a secret as we can. It means hiding. Fundamentally, we're saying,

'I can't share what I am doing with others.'.

During recovery, your addiction is out in the open - at least to some people. However, does this means that living a secret life is over? Do you still have the feeling that people can't find out? And do you still hide a dark side, even from yourself? True healing starts with accepting yourself. The first step in this process is being aware of what is hidden beneath the surface. *What is the monster under your bed?*

> Hang on to your youthful enthusiasms --
> you'll be able to use them better when you're older.

Seneca

DATE: _____-_____-_____

If I did this, today would be great.

_____

_____

How could I help myself today?

_____

_____

_____

_____

My affirmation for today.

_____

_____

EVENING

What did I learn today?

_____

_____

_____

_____

What made me grateful today?

_____

_____

_____

> **The most common way people give up their power**
> **is by thinking they don't have any.**
>
> Alice Walker

DATE: _____-_____-_____

If I did this, today would be great.

_____

_____

How could I help myself today?

_____

_____

_____

_____

My affirmation for today.

_____

_____

EVENING

What did I learn today?

_____

_____

_____

_____

What made me grateful today?

_____

_____

_____

> Remember, remember, this is now, and now, and now.
> Live it, feel it, cling to it.
>
> Sylvia Plath

DATE: _____-_____-_____

If I did this, today would be great.

_____

_____

How could I help myself today?

_____

_____

_____

_____

My affirmation for today.

_____

_____

EVENING

What did I learn today?

_____

_____

_____

_____

What made me grateful today?

_____

_____

_____

Very few of us
are what we seem.

Agatha Christie

DATE: _____-_____-_____

If I did this, today would be great.

_____

_____

How could I help myself today?

_____

_____

_____

_____

My affirmation for today.

_____

_____

EVENING

What did I learn today?

_____

_____

_____

_____

What made me grateful today?

_____

_____

_____

> ... the secret in handling fear is to move yourself from a
> position of pain to a position of power.

Susan Jeffers

DATE: _____-_____-_____

If I did this, today would be great.

_____

_____

How could I help myself today?

_____

_____

_____

_____

My affirmation for today.

_____

_____

EVENING

What did I learn today?

_____

_____

_____

_____

_____

What made me grateful today?

_____

_____

_____

Life's under no obligation
to give us what we expect.

Margaret Mitchell

Date: _____-_____-_____

If I did this, today would be great.

_____

_____

How could I help myself today?

_____

_____

_____

_____

My affirmation for today.

_____

_____

EVENING

What did I learn today?

_____

_____

_____

_____

What made me grateful today?

_____

_____

_____

This is your life
and it's ending one moment at a time.

Chuck Palahniuk

DATE: _____-_____-_____

If I did this, today would be great.

_____

_____

How could I help myself today?

_____

_____

_____

_____

My affirmation for today.

_____

_____

EVENING

What did I learn today?

_____

_____

_____

_____

What made me grateful today?

_____

_____

_____

Enjoying Life

Treat yourself this week. Make an effort to enjoy life. Take a breath, smile and experience the joy of living. There is enough time to solve your problems, have the tears and examine your worries. Try a different perspective every once in a while. See the beauty. Experience the moment. Dance, sing, make love, talk, laugh, live. Live. Live.

> People generally see what they look for,
> and hear what they listen for.

Harper Lee

DATE: _____-_____-_____

If I did this, today would be great.

_____

_____

How could I help myself today?

_____

_____

_____

_____

My affirmation for today.

_____

_____

EVENING

What did I learn today?

_____

_____

_____

_____

What made me grateful today?

_____

_____

_____

> To establish that a rule is likely to be true,
> one must try to prove it false.

Stuart Sutherland

DATE: ____-____-_____

If I did this, today would be great.

_____

_____

How could I help myself today?

_____

_____

_____

_____

My affirmation for today.

_____

_____

EVENING

What did I learn today?

_____

_____

_____

_____

What made me grateful today?

_____

_____

_____

> The key is to keep company only with people who uplift you, whose presence calls forth your best.

Epictetus

DATE: _____-_____-_____

If I did this, today would be great.

_____

_____

How could I help myself today?

_____

_____

_____

_____

My affirmation for today.

_____

_____

EVENING

What did I learn today?

_____

_____

_____

_____

_____

What made me grateful today?

_____

_____

_____

The weak can never forgive.
Forgiveness is the attribute of the strong.

Mahatma Gandhi

DATE: _____-_____-_____

If I did this, today would be great.

_____

_____

How could I help myself today?

_____

_____

_____

_____

My affirmation for today.

_____

_____

EVENING

What did I learn today?

_____

_____

_____

_____

What made me grateful today?

_____

_____

_____

It always seems impossible
until it's done.

Nelson Mandela

DATE: _____-_____-_____

If I did this, today would be great.

_____

_____

How could I help myself today?

_____

_____

_____

_____

My affirmation for today.

_____

_____

EVENING

What did I learn today?

_____

_____

_____

_____

What made me grateful today?

_____

_____

_____

> Have enough courage to trust love one more time
> and always one more time.
>
> Maya Angelou

DATE: ____-____-_____

If I did this, today would be great.

_____

_____

How could I help myself today?

_____

_____

_____

_____

My affirmation for today.

_____

_____

EVENING

What did I learn today?

_____

_____

_____

_____

What made me grateful today?

_____

_____

_____

Life is beautiful
if you are on the road to somewhere.

Orhan Pamuk

DATE: _____-_____-_____

If I did this, today would be great.

_____

_____

How could I help myself today?

_____

_____

_____

My affirmation for today.

_____

_____

EVENING

What did I learn today?

_____

_____

_____

_____

What made me grateful today?

_____

_____

_____

Goals

I was never a person for making long term goals. Yes, I had extensive and intimidating to-do-lists, but that was about it. When I chose to stay sober, some long forgotten dreams came back. I saw that there were still possibilities to achieve what I wanted in life. By carefully planning out three month and six month goals, and taking small steps every day, I started to see results. More importantly, I recognized a sense of control that improved my self-esteem and feeling of confidence.

The delicious breath of rain
was in the air.

Kate Chopin

DATE: _____-_____-_____

If I did this, today would be great.

How could I help myself today?

My affirmation for today.

EVENING

What did I learn today?

What made me grateful today?

Of all the judgments we pass in life, none is more important than the judgment we pass on ourselves.

Nathaniel Branden

DATE: _____-_____-_____

If I did this, today would be great.

_____

_____

How could I help myself today?

_____

_____

_____

My affirmation for today.

_____

_____

EVENING

What did I learn today?

_____

_____

_____

_____

What made me grateful today?

_____

_____

_____

If you want to overcome the whole world, overcome yourself.

Fyodor Dostoyevsky

DATE: _____-_____-_____

If I did this, today would be great.

_____

_____

How could I help myself today?

_____

_____

_____

_____

My affirmation for today.

_____

_____

EVENING

What did I learn today?

_____

_____

_____

_____

What made me grateful today?

_____

_____

_____

Forever
is composed of nows.

Emily Dickinson

DATE: _____-_____-_____

If I did this, today would be great.

_____

_____

How could I help myself today?

_____

_____

_____

_____

My affirmation for today.

_____

_____

EVENING

What did I learn today?

_____

_____

_____

_____

What made me grateful today?

_____

_____

_____

You attract
what you need like a lover

Gertrude Stein

DATE: _____-_____-_____

If I did this, today would be great.

_____

_____

How could I help myself today?

_____

_____

_____

_____

My affirmation for today.

_____

_____

EVENING

What did I learn today?

_____

_____

_____

_____

What made me grateful today?

_____

_____

_____

> Rivers know this: there is no hurry.
> We shall get there some day.

A.A. Milne

DATE: ____-____-_____

If I did this, today would be great.

_____

_____

How could I help myself today?

_____

_____

_____

My affirmation for today.

_____

_____

EVENING

What did I learn today?

_____

_____

_____

_____

What made me grateful today?

_____

_____

_____

> **Beauty is a question of optics.**
> **All sight is illusion.**
>
> Joyce Carol Oates

DATE: ____-____-_____

If I did this, today would be great.

How could I help myself today?

My affirmation for today.

EVENING

What did I learn today?

What made me grateful today?

Health

What is one thing you could do to improve your health today? And this week? Try to ask yourself this question repeatedly. Make it a daily habit and plan it in your calendar. Even small actions, such as drinking a smoothie a day or having at least five glasses of water, could make a significant difference over time. With better health comes more energy, a more positive attitude and a feeling of self-confidence. Take good care of your temple, and give it the care it deserves.

**You can have it all.
Just not all at once.**

Oprah Winfrey

DATE: _____-_____-_____

If I did this, today would be great.

_____
_____

How could I help myself today?

_____
_____
_____
_____

My affirmation for today.

_____
_____

EVENING

What did I learn today?

_____
_____
_____
_____

What made me grateful today?

_____
_____
_____

> Whatever you're meant to do, do it now.
> The conditions are always impossible.

Doris Lessing

DATE: ____-____-_____

If I did this, today would be great.

How could I help myself today?

My affirmation for today.

EVENING

What did I learn today?

What made me grateful today?

How much more grievous are the consequences of anger than the causes of it.

Marcus Aurelius

DATE: _____-_____-_____

If I did this, today would be great.

_____

_____

How could I help myself today?

_____

_____

_____

_____

My affirmation for today.

_____

_____

EVENING

What did I learn today?

_____

_____

_____

_____

_____

What made me grateful today?

_____

_____

_____

Time
is how you spend your love.

Zadie Smith

DATE: _____-_____-_____

If I did this, today would be great.

_____

_____

How could I help myself today?

_____

_____

_____

_____

My affirmation for today.

_____

_____

EVENING

What did I learn today?

_____

_____

_____

_____

What made me grateful today?

_____

_____

_____

> **It is better to fail in originality than to succeed in imitation.**
>
> Herman Melville

DATE: _____-_____-_____

If I did this, today would be great.

_____

_____

How could I help myself today?

_____

_____

_____

_____

My affirmation for today.

_____

_____

EVENING

What did I learn today?

_____

_____

_____

_____

_____

What made me grateful today?

_____

_____

_____

The invisible is only another unexplored country, a brave new world.

Angela Carter

DATE: _____-_____-_____

If I did this, today would be great.

_____

_____

How could I help myself today?

_____

_____

_____

_____

My affirmation for today.

_____

_____

EVENING

What did I learn today?

_____

_____

_____

_____

What made me grateful today?

_____

_____

_____

Where wisdom reigns,
there is no conflict between thinking and feeling.

Carl Gustav Jung

DATE: ____-____-_____

If I did this, today would be great.

How could I help myself today?

My affirmation for today.

EVENING

What did I learn today?

What made me grateful today?

Gratitude

"Gratitude can transform common days into Thanksgivings, turn routine jobs into joy and change ordinary opportunities into blessings."
William Arthur Ward, American Author (1921 - 1994)

Try to make a list in the following days for all the things you're grateful for. A list of at least 50 things. Make this your go to list, so you have something to fall back on when life is tough.

> Don't judge each day by the harvest you reap
> but by the seeds that you plant.

Robert Louis Stevenson

DATE: ____-____-_____

If I did this, today would be great.

_____

_____

How could I help myself today?

_____

_____

_____

_____

My affirmation for today.

_____

_____

EVENING

What did I learn today?

_____

_____

_____

_____

What made me grateful today?

_____

_____

_____

None but ourselves can free our minds.

Bob Marley

DATE: ____-____-_____

If I did this, today would be great.

_____

_____

How could I help myself today?

_____

_____

_____

_____

My affirmation for today.

_____

_____

EVENING

What did I learn today?

_____

_____

_____

_____

What made me grateful today?

_____

_____

_____

> Sometimes our light goes out, but is blown again into instant flame by an encounter with another human being.

Albert Schweitzer

DATE: _____-_____-_____

If I did this, today would be great.

_____
_____

How could I help myself today?

_____
_____
_____
_____

My affirmation for today.

_____
_____

EVENING

What did I learn today?

_____
_____
_____
_____

What made me grateful today?

_____
_____
_____

> Clouds come floating into my life, no longer to carry rain
> or usher storm, but to add color to my sunset sky.

Rabindranath Tagore

DATE: _____-_____-_____

If I did this, today would be great.

_____

_____

How could I help myself today?

_____

_____

_____

_____

My affirmation for today.

_____

_____

EVENING

What did I learn today?

_____

_____

_____

_____

_____

What made me grateful today?

_____

_____

_____

Don't be afraid of your fears. They're not there to scare you.
They're there to let you know that something is worth it.

C. JoyBell C.

Date: _____-_____-_____

If I did this, today would be great.

_____
_____

How could I help myself today?

_____
_____
_____
_____

My affirmation for today.

_____
_____

EVENING

What did I learn today?

_____
_____
_____
_____
_____

What made me grateful today?

_____
_____
_____

All the darkness in the world cannot extinguish the light of a single candle.

St. Francis Of Assisi

DATE: ____-____-_____

If I did this, today would be great.

_____

_____

How could I help myself today?

_____

_____

_____

_____

My affirmation for today.

_____

_____

EVENING

What did I learn today?

_____

_____

_____

_____

What made me grateful today?

_____

_____

_____

> If only we'd stop trying to be happy,
> we could have a pretty good time.
>
> Edith Wharton

DATE: _____-_____-_____

If I did this, today would be great.

_____

_____

How could I help myself today?

_____

_____

_____

My affirmation for today.

_____

_____

EVENING

What did I learn today?

_____

_____

_____

_____

What made me grateful today?

_____

_____

_____

Identity

You're worthless.

Those words were echoing through my mind during my drinking years. I felt small. A tiny, breakable child. What do you do with something that is worthless? You throw it away. You destruct it. My drinking was the act of breaking my worthless self. Changing your beliefs about yourself is critical in recovery. Throw off the chains of your negative beliefs.

They're not worth it.

If you are irritated by every rub,
how will your mirror be polished?

Rumi

DATE: ____-____-_____

If I did this, today would be great.

_____

_____

How could I help myself today?

_____

_____

_____

_____

My affirmation for today.

_____

_____

EVENING

What did I learn today?

_____

_____

_____

_____

_____

What made me grateful today?

_____

_____

_____

When people don't express themselves,
they die one piece at a time.

Laurie Halse Anderson

DATE: ____-____-_____

If I did this, today would be great.

_____

_____

How could I help myself today?

_____

_____

_____

_____

My affirmation for today.

_____

_____

EVENING

What did I learn today?

_____

_____

_____

_____

_____

What made me grateful today?

_____

_____

_____

The most beautiful things in the world
cannot be seen or touched, they are felt with the heart.

Antoine de Saint-Exupéry

DATE: ____-____-_____

If I did this, today would be great.

How could I help myself today?

My affirmation for today.

EVENING

What did I learn today?

What made me grateful today?

What's the good of living
if you don't try a few things?

Charles M. Schulz

DATE: ____-____-_____

If I did this, today would be great.

_____

_____

How could I help myself today?

_____

_____

_____

_____

My affirmation for today.

_____

_____

EVENING

What did I learn today?

_____

_____

_____

_____

_____

What made me grateful today?

_____

_____

_____

> There was another life that I might have had,
> but I am having this one.

Kazuo Ishiguro

DATE: ____-____-_____

If I did this, today would be great.

_____

_____

How could I help myself today?

_____

_____

_____

_____

My affirmation for today.

_____

_____

EVENING

What did I learn today?

_____

_____

_____

_____

What made me grateful today?

_____

_____

_____

We cannot change anything
unless we accept it.

Carl Gustav Jung

DATE: _____-_____-_____

If I did this, today would be great.

_____

_____

How could I help myself today?

_____

_____

_____

_____

My affirmation for today.

_____

_____

EVENING

What did I learn today?

_____

_____

_____

_____

What made me grateful today?

_____

_____

_____

> **If you think you are too small to make a difference,**
> **try sleeping with a mosquito.**
>
> The Dalai Lama

DATE: _____-_____-_____

If I did this, today would be great.

_____
_____

How could I help myself today?

_____
_____
_____
_____

My affirmation for today.

_____
_____

EVENING

What did I learn today?

_____
_____
_____
_____
_____

What made me grateful today?

_____
_____
_____

Happiness

What if happiness wasn't a big, fancy and far away dream? A perception change. Pay attention and see the beauty. Pay attention and recognize your strengths. Connect, smile, pick yourself up. Happiness isn't far away, it's a daily act.

There are two ways of spreading light: to be
The candle or the mirror that reflects it.

Edith Wharton

DATE: ____-____-_____

If I did this, today would be great.

How could I help myself today?

My affirmation for today.

EVENING

What did I learn today?

What made me grateful today?

> Remember, darkness does not always equate to evil,
> just as light does not always bring good.
>
> P.C. Cast

DATE: ____-____-_____

If I did this, today would be great.

_____

_____

How could I help myself today?

_____

_____

_____

_____

My affirmation for today.

_____

_____

EVENING

What did I learn today?

_____

_____

_____

_____

_____

What made me grateful today?

_____

_____

_____

> **Go on with what your heart tells you,**
> **or you will lose all.**
>
> Rick Riordan

DATE: ____-____-_____

If I did this, today would be great.

_____

_____

How could I help myself today?

_____

_____

_____

My affirmation for today.

_____

_____

EVENING

What did I learn today?

_____

_____

_____

_____

What made me grateful today?

_____

_____

_____

> There must be those among whom we can sit down
> and weep and still be counted as warriors.

Adrienne Rich

DATE: _____-_____-_____

If I did this, today would be great.

_____

_____

How could I help myself today?

_____

_____

_____

_____

My affirmation for today.

_____

_____

EVENING

What did I learn today?

_____

_____

_____

_____

_____

What made me grateful today?

_____

_____

_____

> When one tugs at a single thing in nature,
> he finds it attached to the rest of the world.
>
> John Muir

DATE: _____-_____-_____

If I did this, today would be great.

_____

_____

How could I help myself today?

_____

_____

_____

_____

My affirmation for today.

_____

_____

EVENING

What did I learn today?

_____

_____

_____

_____

_____

What made me grateful today?

_____

_____

_____

> I don't think of all the misery,
> but of the beauty that still remains.

Anne Frank

DATE: _____-_____-_____

If I did this, today would be great.

_____

_____

How could I help myself today?

_____

_____

_____

_____

My affirmation for today.

_____

_____

EVENING

What did I learn today?

_____

_____

_____

_____

_____

What made me grateful today?

_____

_____

_____

Trees that are slow to grow
bear the best fruit.

Moliere

DATE: _____-_____-_____

If I did this, today would be great.

_____

_____

How could I help myself today?

_____

_____

_____

_____

My affirmation for today.

_____

_____

EVENING

What did I learn today?

_____

_____

_____

_____

_____

What made me grateful today?

_____

_____

_____

Hold still

I was constantly escaping, chasing the next sip. Finding all sort of activities to run away from myself. Stop chasing and find out what is so scary. Because if you don't you will never find your spot.

> ## The question is not what you look at,
> ## but what you see.
>
> Henry David Thoreau

DATE: ____-____-_____

If I did this, today would be great.

_____

_____

How could I help myself today?

_____

_____

_____

_____

My affirmation for today.

_____

_____

EVENING

What did I learn today?

_____

_____

_____

_____

_____

What made me grateful today?

_____

_____

_____

> Keep your face always toward the sunshine -
> and shadows will fall behind you.

Walt Whitman

DATE: ____-____-_____

If I did this, today would be great.

_____

_____

How could I help myself today?

_____

_____

_____

My affirmation for today.

_____

EVENING

What did I learn today?

_____

_____

_____

_____

What made me grateful today?

_____

_____

_____

Whatever you can do or dream you can, begin it.
Boldness has genius, power and magic in it!

John Anster

DATE: ____-____-_____

If I did this, today would be great.

How could I help myself today?

My affirmation for today.

EVENING

What did I learn today?

What made me grateful today?

I am a part
of all that I have met.

Alfred Tennyson

DATE: _____-_____-_____

If I did this, today would be great.

_____

_____

How could I help myself today?

_____

_____

_____

_____

My affirmation for today.

_____

_____

EVENING

What did I learn today?

_____

_____

_____

_____

_____

What made me grateful today?

_____

_____

_____

Wanting to be someone else
is a waste of the person you are.

Marilyn Monroe

DATE: ____-____-_____

If I did this, today would be great.

How could I help myself today?

My affirmation for today.

EVENING

What did I learn today?

What made me grateful today?

> I have never met a man so ignorant
> that I couldn't learn something from him.

Galileo Galilei

DATE: _____-_____-_____

If I did this, today would be great.

_____

_____

How could I help myself today?

_____

_____

_____

My affirmation for today.

_____

EVENING

What did I learn today?

_____

_____

_____

What made me grateful today?

_____

_____

Happiness is not the absence of problems, it's the ability to deal with them.

Steve Maraboli

DATE: _____-_____-_____

If I did this, today would be great.

_____
_____

How could I help myself today?

_____
_____
_____
_____

My affirmation for today.

_____
_____

EVENING

What did I learn today?

_____
_____
_____
_____

What made me grateful today?

_____
_____
_____

Meditation

Are negative thoughts running your show? Learn to calm the mind. Control what is yours, your life. Meditation is a fine way to learn this. Try it out and see calmness enriching your life.

Sometimes you wake up. Sometimes the fall kills you.
And sometimes, when you fall, you fly.

Neil Gaiman

DATE: _____-_____-_____

If I did this, today would be great.

How could I help myself today?

My affirmation for today.

EVENING

What did I learn today?

What made me grateful today?

Don't think or judge,
just listen.

Sarah Dessen

DATE: ____-____-_____

If I did this, today would be great.

_____

_____

How could I help myself today?

_____

_____

_____

_____

My affirmation for today.

_____

_____

EVENING

What did I learn today?

_____

_____

_____

_____

_____

What made me grateful today?

_____

_____

_____

You cannot find peace
by avoiding life.

Michael Cunningham

DATE: ____-____-_____

If I did this, today would be great.

_____

_____

How could I help myself today?

_____

_____

_____

_____

My affirmation for today.

_____

_____

EVENING

What did I learn today?

_____

_____

_____

_____

What made me grateful today?

_____

_____

_____

161

All we have to decide
is what to do with the time that is given us.

J.R.R. Tolkien

DATE: _____-_____-_____

If I did this, today would be great.

_____

_____

How could I help myself today?

_____

_____

_____

_____

My affirmation for today.

_____

_____

EVENING

What did I learn today?

_____

_____

_____

_____

_____

What made me grateful today?

_____

_____

_____

> Vocabularies are crossing circles and loops. We are defined
> by the lines we choose to cross or to be confined by.

A.S. Byatt

Date: ____-____-_____

If I did this, today would be great.

_____

_____

How could I help myself today?

_____

_____

_____

My affirmation for today.

_____

_____

EVENING

What did I learn today?

_____

_____

_____

_____

_____

What made me grateful today?

_____

_____

_____

The more one judges,
the less one loves.

Honoré de Balzac

DATE: ____-____-_____

If I did this, today would be great.

_____

_____

How could I help myself today?

_____

_____

_____

My affirmation for today.

_____

_____

EVENING

What did I learn today?

_____

_____

_____

_____

What made me grateful today?

_____

_____

_____

> In the depth of winter, I finally learned
> that within me there lay an invincible summer.
>
> Albert Camus

DATE: ____-____-_____

If I did this, today would be great.

_____
_____

How could I help myself today?

_____
_____
_____
_____

My affirmation for today.

_____

EVENING

What did I learn today?

_____
_____
_____
_____
_____

What made me grateful today?

_____
_____
_____

Together

"If you want to go fast, go alone.
If you want go far, go together."
African proverb

If you're too much in your own head, you forget
sometimes that there is a whole world out there. Open
your eyes, meet the other. Treat him or her with care and
respect. Why don't you smile? A kind word can make
someone's day.

> Nobody has ever measured, not even poets,
> how much the heart can hold.

Zelda Fitzgerald

DATE: ____-____-_____

If I did this, today would be great.

_____

_____

How could I help myself today?

_____

_____

_____

_____

My affirmation for today.

_____

_____

EVENING

What did I learn today?

_____

_____

_____

_____

_____

What made me grateful today?

_____

_____

_____

If you don't try,
nothing ever changes.

Elena Ferrante

DATE: ____-____-_____

If I did this, today would be great.

How could I help myself today?

My affirmation for today.

EVENING

What did I learn today?

What made me grateful today?

> We should all start to live before we get too old.
> Fear is stupid. So are regrets.

Marilyn Monroe

DATE: _____-_____-_____

If I did this, today would be great.

_____

_____

How could I help myself today?

_____

_____

_____

_____

My affirmation for today.

_____

_____

EVENING

What did I learn today?

_____

_____

_____

_____

_____

What made me grateful today?

_____

_____

_____

And those who were seen dancing were thought to be insane
by those who could not hear the music.

Friedrich Nietzsche

Date: ____-____-_____

If I did this, today would be great.

How could I help myself today?

My affirmation for today.

EVENING

What did I learn today?

What made me grateful today?

> I have a huge and savage conscience
> that won't let me get away with things.

Octavia E. Butler

DATE: ____-____-_____

If I did this, today would be great.

How could I help myself today?

My affirmation for today.

EVENING

What did I learn today?

What made me grateful today?

We loved with a love
that was more than love.

Edgar Allen Poe

DATE: ____-____-_____

If I did this, today would be great.

How could I help myself today?

My affirmation for today.

EVENING

What did I learn today?

What made me grateful today?

Some people care too much.
I think it's called love.

A.A. Milne

DATE: _____-_____-_____

If I did this, today would be great.

_____

_____

How could I help myself today?

_____

_____

_____

My affirmation for today.

_____

_____

EVENING

What did I learn today?

_____

_____

_____

_____

What made me grateful today?

_____

_____

_____

Relapse

There are hardly any roads without obstacles. Life has a way to give us the lesson we need, or that we deserve. Recovery can be hard and painful. Strings of moments can lead to relapse. The craving for alcohol too strong. An old destructive friend, seemingly the solution for all of your problems.

The majority of people who go for sobriety will have one or multiple relapses. Don't be encouraged when it happened to you. Dust off your shoulders. Have faith. Dry your tears and gently pick yourself up. Feel that the Universe has a different purpose for you. Take a good look at the many steps that lead to your addiction. Be aware of your pitfalls.

Close the road that lead to destruction.

Your task is not to seek for love, but merely to seek and find all the barriers within yourself that you have built against it.

Rumi

DATE: ____-____-_____

If I did this, today would be great.

_____

_____

How could I help myself today?

_____

_____

_____

My affirmation for today.

_____

EVENING

What did I learn today?

_____

_____

_____

What made me grateful today?

_____

_____

_____

Every saint has a past,
and every sinner has a future.

Oscar Wilde

DATE: ____-____-_____

If I did this, today would be great.

_____

_____

How could I help myself today?

_____

_____

_____

My affirmation for today.

_____

_____

EVENING

What did I learn today?

_____

_____

_____

_____

What made me grateful today?

_____

_____

_____

> **If you look for perfection,**
> **you'll never be content.**
>
> Leo Tolstoy

DATE: _____-_____-_____

If I did this, today would be great.

_____

_____

How could I help myself today?

_____

_____

_____

_____

My affirmation for today.

_____

_____

EVENING

What did I learn today?

_____

_____

_____

_____

_____

What made me grateful today?

_____

_____

_____

If you did not want much,
there was plenty.

Harper Lee

DATE: _____-_____-_____

If I did this, today would be great.

_____
_____

How could I help myself today?

_____
_____
_____
_____

My affirmation for today.

_____
_____

EVENING

What did I learn today?

_____
_____
_____
_____
_____

What made me grateful today?

_____
_____
_____

Sometimes, one wants to have the illusion
that one is making ones own life, out of one's own resources.

Zadie Smith

DATE: ____-____-_____

If I did this, today would be great.

How could I help myself today?

My affirmation for today.

EVENING

What did I learn today?

What made me grateful today?

People do not wish to appear foolish; to avoid the appearance of foolishness, they are willing to remain actually fools.

Alice Walker

DATE: ____-____-_____

If I did this, today would be great.

_____

_____

How could I help myself today?

_____

_____

_____

My affirmation for today.

_____

_____

EVENING

What did I learn today?

_____

_____

_____

_____

_____

What made me grateful today?

_____

_____

_____

Find ecstasy in life;
the mere sense of living is joy enough.

Emily Dickinson

DATE: _____-_____-_____

If I did this, today would be great.

_____

_____

How could I help myself today?

_____

_____

_____

_____

My affirmation for today.

_____

_____

EVENING

What did I learn today?

_____

_____

_____

_____

What made me grateful today?

_____

_____

_____

Changes

"People are not meant to be on this earth just to fight an addiction."
C.W. V. Straaten, The Addiction Recovery Workbook

If you want to escape the life that leads to alcoholism, you have to make changes. Any changes. Start with new, positive and encouraging routines. Play it small. For example by making your bed in the morning and drinking a smoothie every day. Small steps to show yourself that you can keep a commitment.

> ## Our life is frittered away by detail.
> ## Simplify, simplify.
>
> Henry David Thoreau

DATE: ____-____-_____

If I did this, today would be great.

_____

_____

How could I help myself today?

_____

_____

_____

_____

My affirmation for today.

_____

_____

EVENING

What did I learn today?

_____

_____

_____

_____

_____

What made me grateful today?

_____

_____

_____

Things can change
in a day.

Arundhati Roy

DATE: ____-____-_____

If I did this, today would be great.

_____

_____

How could I help myself today?

_____

_____

_____

_____

My affirmation for today.

_____

_____

EVENING

What did I learn today?

_____

_____

_____

_____

_____

What made me grateful today?

_____

_____

_____

> **In all chaos there is a cosmos,
> in all disorder a secret order.**
>
> Carl Gustav Jung

DATE: _____-_____-_____

If I did this, today would be great.

_____

_____

How could I help myself today?

_____

_____

_____

_____

My affirmation for today.

_____

_____

EVENING

What did I learn today?

_____

_____

_____

_____

_____

What made me grateful today?

_____

_____

_____

> You have to pick the places
> you don't walk away from.
>
> Joan Didion

DATE: ____-____-_____

If I did this, today would be great.

_____
_____

How could I help myself today?

_____
_____
_____
_____

My affirmation for today.

_____
_____

EVENING

What did I learn today?

_____
_____
_____
_____
_____

What made me grateful today?

_____
_____
_____

> To persevere with the will to understand in the face of obstacles is the heroism of consciousness.
>
> Nathaniel Branden

DATE: _____-_____-_____

If I did this, today would be great.

_____

_____

How could I help myself today?

_____

_____

_____

My affirmation for today.

_____

EVENING

What did I learn today?

_____

_____

_____

_____

What made me grateful today?

_____

_____

_____

I will vanish in the morning light;
I was only an invention of darkness.

Angela Carter

DATE: ____-____-_____

If I did this, today would be great.

_____

_____

How could I help myself today?

_____

_____

_____

My affirmation for today.

_____

_____

EVENING

What did I learn today?

_____

_____

_____

_____

What made me grateful today?

_____

_____

_____

Everything is interesting
if you know how to work on it.

Elena Ferrante

DATE: ____-____-_____

If I did this, today would be great.

_____

_____

How could I help myself today?

_____

_____

_____

_____

My affirmation for today.

_____

_____

EVENING

What did I learn today?

_____

_____

_____

_____

What made me grateful today?

_____

_____

_____

Spirituality

Did you ever have the feeling during your recovery, or the darkest moments, that in a sense you were carried? Carried by a divine being, or the universe itself?

I personally believe that we don't have to bear our pain all by ourselves. For me my recovery journey changed when I believed that this was the path set out for me. Faith that I was meant for something different than suffering and drinking cheap bottles of wine and vodka.

Let faith be your new foundation, instead of evil and destructive uncertainties.

YOUR OWN FINAL THOUGHTS

Write down your own Final Thoughts.

ABOUT THE AUTHOR

Joanne Edmund is the author of *'Quit Drinking! An Inspiring Recovery Workbook.'* You can purchase this book here, www.amazon.com/gp/product/1719450358

In this book she wrote courageously about her struggle with alcoholism. With her recovery workbook she helped many to understand and overcome their drinking problem. As a young girl, she always wanted to be a writer. In *Quit Drinking* she wrote:

"Fairy tales, in old books, seemed to tell of a world far away from my own. A fine, fine world. Many years later, I am a grown-up woman and fairy tales still get me from time to time. Though the first book I'll publish is not one of kissing teenagers or magic elves, it's about the truth. About my addiction and what I did to overcome it. Now, under a pen name for substantial reasons, I am ready to make my dream come true. To become a writer. To tell you, the reader, that recovery, the fairy tale of every problem drinker, is not just a story. It is the one and final truth."

She has the intention to write more self-help books in the future. If you want to contact the author you can send an email to lastingrecovery@yahoo.com. She will read and respond to every email.

The
Sobriety Journal

Made in the USA
Monee, IL
09 September 2019